HANDOUTS
AND
OBLIGATIONS

MW00535182

PETER SCHUMANN

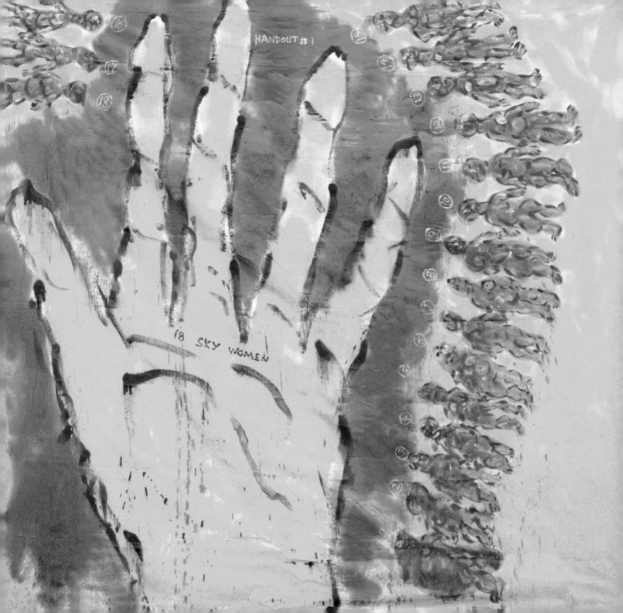

HANDOUT # 2

THE OBLIGATION
To EMBRACE

HANDOUT # 3

OVER-UNDER LIFE PURSUITS OF DWARVES NOT READY FOR ANYTHING BIGGER THAN THE LITTLE

SQUARE PLANET EARTH
DENUNCIATION OBLIGATION

AS YOU FALL

FROM

THE CLIFF

YOU REMEMBER

THE EARTH

SO UNSEEN

BEFORE

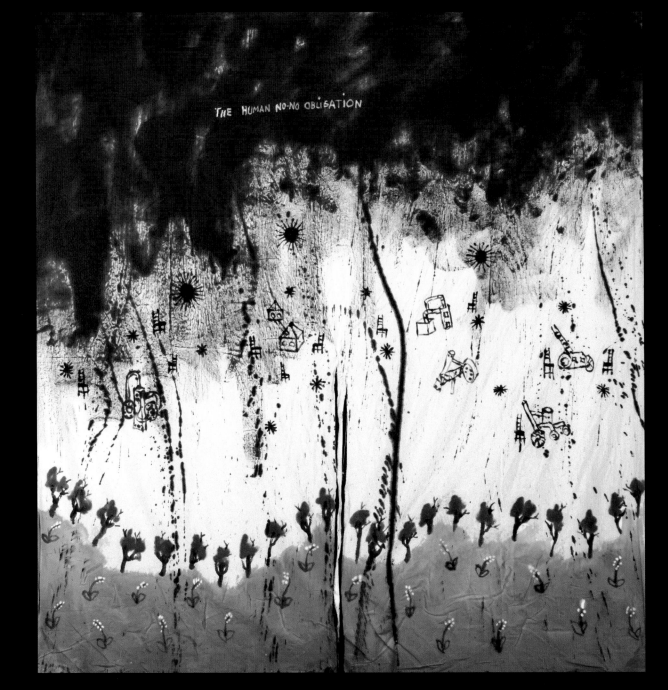

OBLIGATION TO BURN

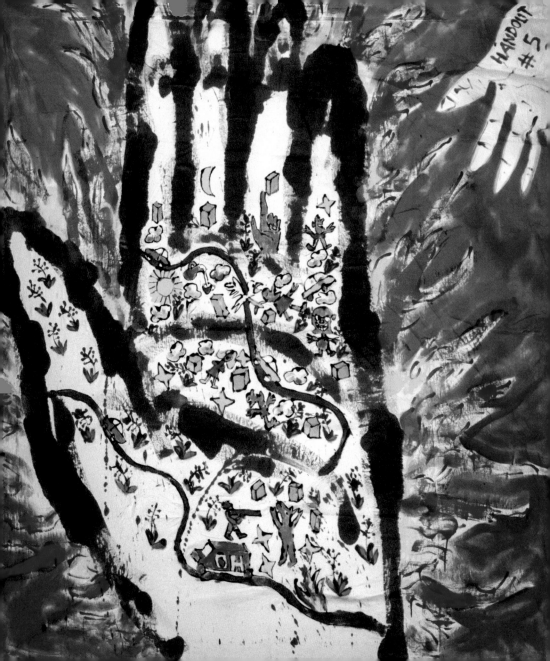

HANDOUT #5

OH!

THE OBLIGATION
TO EXIST

OBLIGATION TO STOP THE DIAGONAL LIFE

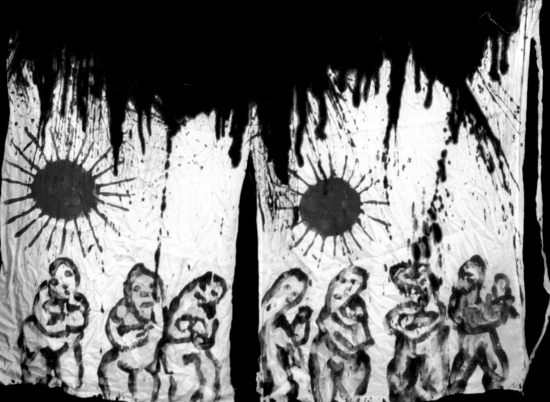

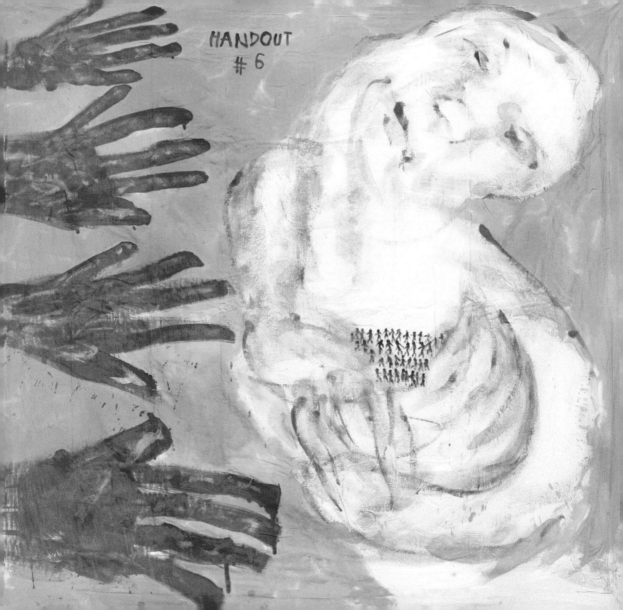

HANDOUT #6

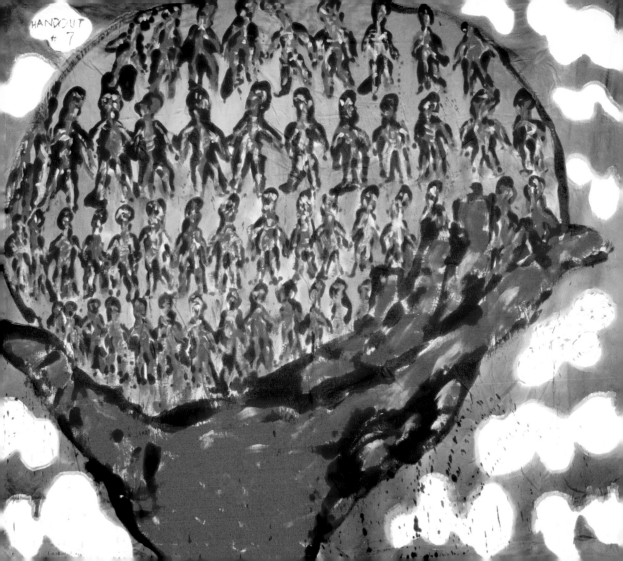

HANDOUT
7

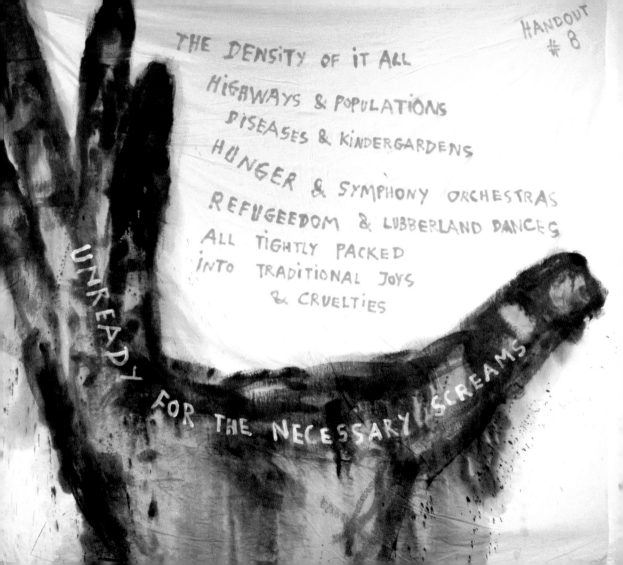

THE DENSITY OF IT ALL
HIGHWAYS & POPULATIONS
DISEASES & KINDERGARDENS
HUNGER & SYMPHONY ORCHESTRAS
REFUGEEDOM & LUBBERLAND DANCES
ALL TIGHTLY PACKED
INTO TRADITIONAL JOYS
& CRUELTIES

UNREADY FOR THE NECESSARY SCREAMS

OBLIGATION

CARRYING NOT

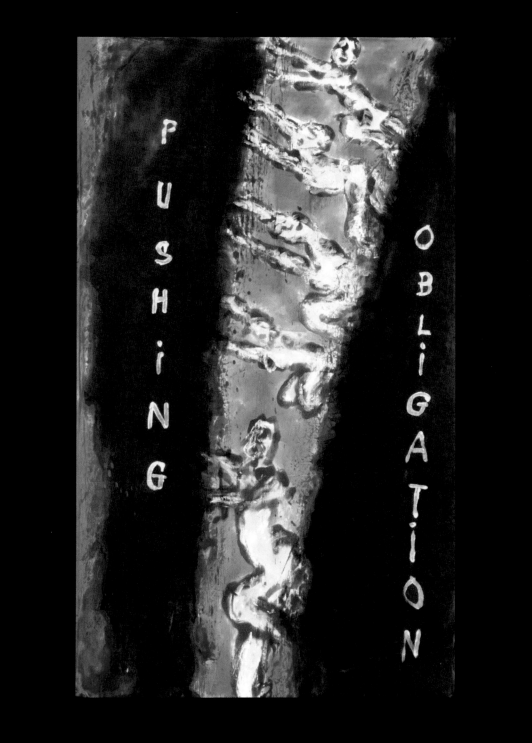

UPSIDEDOWN   OBLIGATION

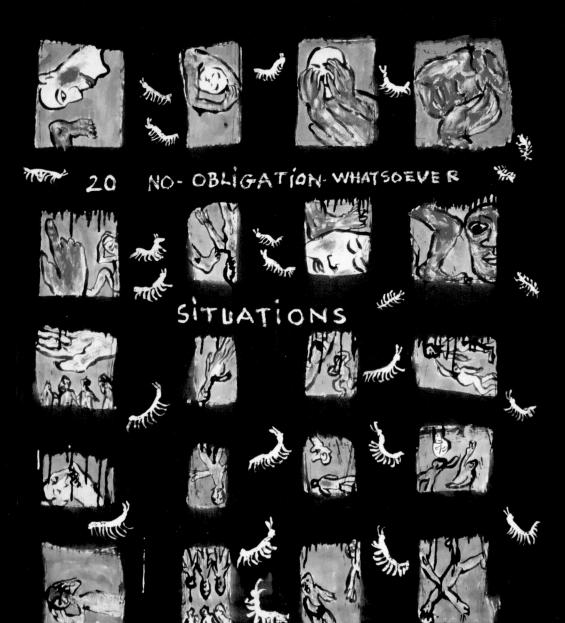

20   NO-OBLIGATION-WHATSOEVER

SITUATIONS

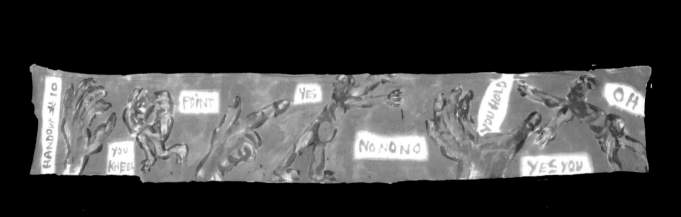

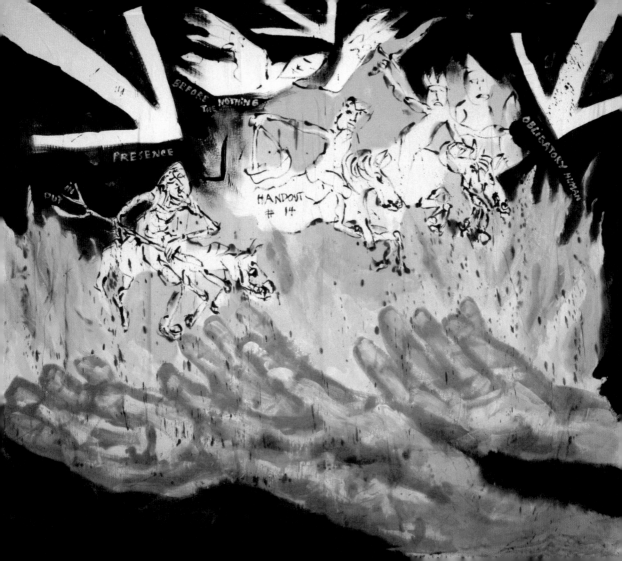

DECLARATION OF LIGHT

LIGHT CANNOT ONLY MEAN THE
OLD LIGHT. WE NEED NEW LIGHT
BECAUSE OF THE EXHAUSTION LIGHT
HAS SUFFERED FROM THE MANY MISUSES
WE HAVE SUBMITTED IT TO

LIGHT IS A QUALITY THAT NEEDS TO BE
OVERHAULED & ADJUSTED TO THE SPECIFIC
DARKNESS OF A SPECIFIC TIME.
EXTRACTED FROM THE ETERNAL SOURCE
LIGHT HAS TO BE INVENTED AGAIN & AGAIN
TO FIGHT HUMAN DARKNESS

HANDOUT
15

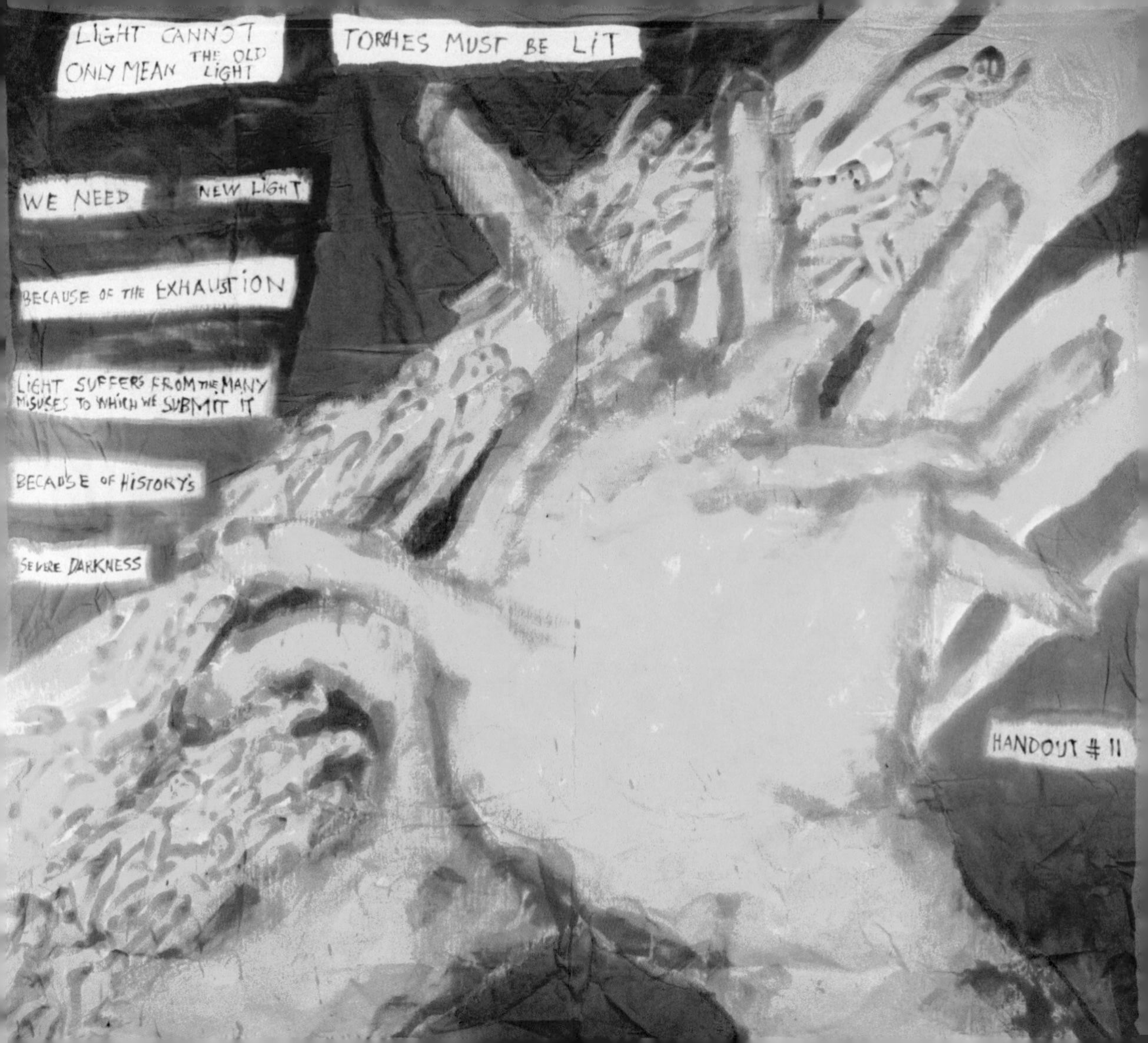

LIGHT CANNOT
ONLY MEAN THE OLD
LIGHT

TORCHES MUST BE LIT

WE NEED   NEW LIGHT

BECAUSE OF THE EXHAUSTION

LIGHT SUFFERS FROM THE MANY
MISUSES TO WHICH WE SUBMIT IT

BECAUSE OF HISTORY'S

SEVERE DARKNESS

HANDOUT # 11

HANDOUT
16

HUMAN SUNRISE DEMONSTRATED BY
UPSIDEDOWN POPULATION

LANDSCAPE OBLIGATION

THE SKY IS THE INSTITUTION
THAT CONTAINS & ISSUES
ALL OF LIFE'S FORMS & IDEAS
& POURS THEM UNTO THE
UNDERNEATH TILL
EVERYTHING IS THERE
& PROLIFERATES & THEN
JUST AS EASILY BURNS IT

OBLIGATION love

NOTHING LESS
NOTHING LESS
NOTHING MORE
NOTHING MORE
NOTHING MORE

LIGHTWORKERS &
DWARVES ARE NEEDED

TO PENETRATE THE
INACCESSIBLE
UNDERGROUND

HANDOUT
#23

HANDOUT
24

THE BYE BYE OBLIGATION

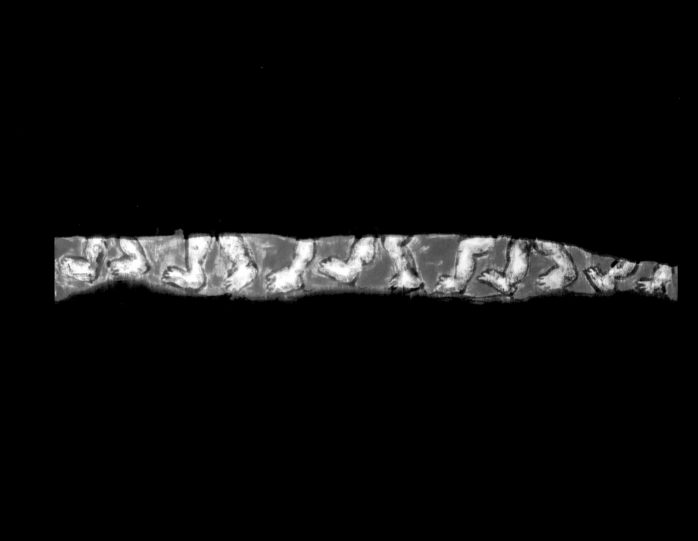

HANDOUT
#25

HANDOUT #26

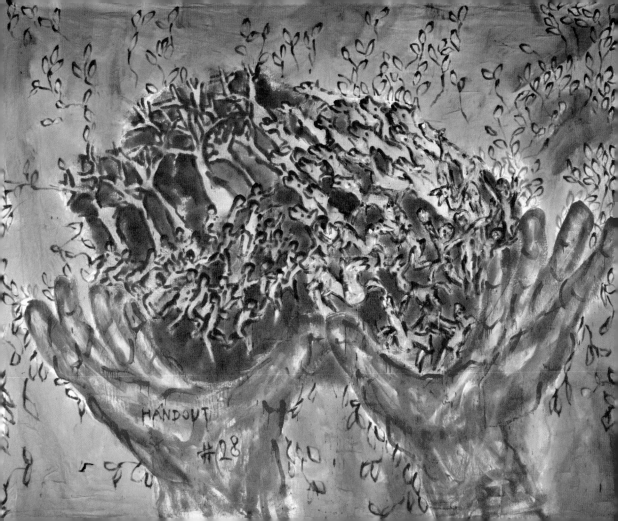

HANDOUT

#28

TO DISTORT
THE CAPITALIST
MODEL OF VAST FAILURE
OF SERVICE TO THE POPULATION

①THE SCREAMING HARRIERS
AND RAVENS UPSET US
INSUFFICIENTLY

②FOR THE IMBALANCE WE
NEED FOR THE MOST
URGENT DISTORTIONS
WHICH CORRECT REALITY

④AND THE INCOMPETENT
HEALTHCARE SCREAMS

③OTHER SCREAMS MUST BE
ADDED: THE POVERTY AND
THE INJUSTICE
SCREAMS

WE THE SCREAMERS
MUST LEARN ALL AVAILABLE
SCREAMING MUSICS;
THAT HUMANITY HAS FOREVER COMPOSED
TO ADDRESS THE MULTIPLE HEARTS
OF MULTIPLE MATTERS

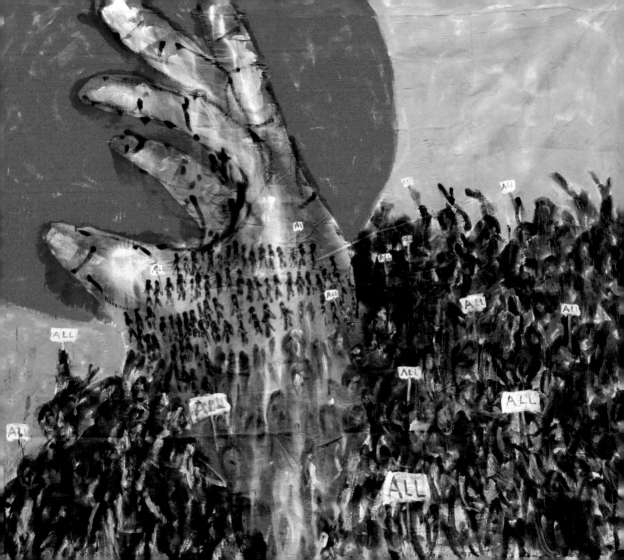

IN MEMORIAM

BURT PORTER (1937-2020)

REMI PAILLARD (1942-2021)

THE OBLIGATION TO SING

OUR YEARS, HOW MANY TIMES HAD THIS HUGE EARTH SUN BEFORE WE MET?
AND THEN HOW LONG WILL IT SPIN ON WHEN WE ARE IN THE SWUNG 'ROUND THE DREAMS OR LONG FORGOTTEN SONGS
OF ALL THE COUNTLESS YEARS THAT HAVE GONE BY. OF ALL THE GROUND GONE LIKE UNGLIMPSED YEARS THAT YET
OURS ARE BUT FEW. SO LET US LOVE EACH OTHER SHALL BE
WHILE WE MAY

CONFRONTED BY COVID, OBLIGATIONS
EASILY GET ANGRY & CALL FOR SERIOUS STOPS
& DISEMBARKMENTS OR ASK THE LIGHTWORKERS
FOR NEW FORMS OF LIGHT & LOVE & SUNRISES
FOR ALL!
THESE REPURPOSED DISCARDED BEDSHEETS
& SCRAPS OF TORN SHEETS (DONATED BY
RICHARD BRIGHAM) WANT TO MITIGATE
PAIN & ENLIGHTEN DARK NIGHTS.
THE PAINT IS LATEX HOUSEPAINT
ACQUIRED AT LOCAL PAINTSALES BY
LINDA ELBOW. EXCERPTS FROM THE
PAINTED BEDSHEET COLLECTION ARE
REGULARLY EXHIBITED IN VERMONT
TOWNS BY ALEXIS SMITH. GARY
PATRICK HARVEY PHOTOGRAPHED THEM.
DONNA BISTER & MARC ESTRIN
CONCEIVED, EDITED & DESIGNED
THE BOOK.
THANK YOU ALL!
Re Schn

PETER SCHUMANN is the founder and director of the Bread & Puppet Theater. Born in Silesia, he was a sculptor and dancer in Germany before moving to the United States in 1961.

OTHER PETER SCHUMANN BOOKS FROM FOMITE

Made in the USA
Middletown, DE
02 May 2022

65142701R00049